CAPTAIN AMERICA

LOOSE NUKE

COLLECTION EDITOR
JENNIFER GRÜNWALD

ASSOCIATE MANAGING EDITOR
ALEX STARBUCK

EDITOR, SPECIAL PROJECTS
MARK D. BEAZLEY

SENIOR EDITOR,
SPECIAL PROJECTS
JEFF YOUNGQUIST

SVP PRINT, SALES
& MARKETING
DAVID GABRIEL

EDITOR IN CHIEF
AXEL ALONSO

CHIEF CREATIVE OFFICER
JOE QUESADA

PUBLISHER
DAN BUCKLEY

LOOSE NUKE

WRITER
RICK REMENDER

ISSUES #11-12 & #14-15
PENCILER
CARLOS PACHECO
INKERS
KLAUS JANSON (#11-12)
& MARIANO TAIBO (#14-15)

ISSUE #13
ARTIST
NIC KLEIN

COLOR ARTISTS
DEAN WHITE
WITH RACHELLE ROSENBERG (#12),
RAIN BEREDO (#15) & VAL STAPLES (#15)

LETTERER
VC'S JOE CARAMAGNA

COVER ART
CARLOS PACHECO & DEAN WHITE (#11-14)
AND JIM CHEUNG & LAURA MARTIN (#15)

ASSISTANT EDITOR
JAKE THOMAS

EDITOR
TOM BREVOORT

CAPTAIN AMERICA CREATED BY JOE SIMON & JACK KIRBY

CAPTAIN AMERICA VOL. 3: LOOSE NUKE. Contains material originally published in magazine form as CAPTAIN AMERICA #11-15. First printing 2014. ISBN# 978-0-7851-8951-0. Published by MARVEL WORLDWIDE, INC., a subsidiary of MARVEL ENTERTAINMENT, LLC. OFFICE OF PUBLICATION: 135 West 50th Street, New York, NY 10020. Copyright © 2013 and 2014 Marvel Characters, Inc. All rights reserved. All characters featured in this issue and the distinctive names and likenesses thereof, and all related indicia are trademarks of Marvel Characters, Inc. No similarity between any of the names, characters, persons, and/or institutions in this magazine with those of any living or dead person or institution is intended, and any such similarity which may exist is purely coincidental. **Printed in the U.S.A.** ALAN FINE, EVP - Office of the President, Marvel Worldwide, Inc. and EVP & CMO Marvel Characters B.V.; DAN BUCKLEY, Publisher & President - Print, Animation & Digital Divisions; JOE QUESADA, Chief Creative Officer; TOM BREVOORT, SVP of Publishing; DAVID BOGART, SVP of Operations & Procurement, Publishing; C.B. CEBULSKI, SVP of Creator & Content Development; DAVID GABRIEL, SVP Print, Sales & Marketing; JIM O'KEEFE, VP of Operations & Logistics; DAN CARR, Executive Director of Publishing Technology; SUSAN CRESPI, Editorial Operations Manager; ALEX MORALES, Publishing Operations Manager; STAN LEE, Chairman Emeritus. For information regarding advertising in Marvel Comics or on Marvel.com, please contact Niza Disla, Director of Marvel Partnerships, at ndisla@marvel.com. For Marvel subscription inquiries, please call 800-217-9158. **Manufactured between 2/7/2014 and 3/24/2014 by R.R. DONNELLEY, INC., SALEM, VA, USA.**

10 9 8 7 6 5 4 3 2 1

During WWII, a secret military experiment turned scrawny Steve Rogers into America's first super-soldier, Captain America. Near the end of the war, Rogers was presumed dead in an explosion over the English Channel.

Decades later, Captain America was found frozen in ice and revived. Steve Rogers awakened to a world he never imagined, a man out of time. He again took up the mantle of Captain America, defending the U.S. and the world from threats of all kinds.

PREVIOUSLY...

At long last, Captain America returned from Dimension Z, battered and weary but alive. With him was Jet Black, Arnim Zola's daughter and Cap's unexpected ally. After a years-long one-man war against his nemesis, Steve finally defeated Zola with Jet's help but at a heavy price: in the final confrontation, Steve lost both his adopted son, Ian, and his lover, Sharon Carter.

After 12 years in Dimension Z, Steve Rogers must reenter a world where he was only gone a moment, once again making him a man out of time.

ELEVEN

MANHATTAN.
THE LOWER EAST SIDE, 1935.

I'M SORRY, STEVE.

THERE'S NOTHING MORE I CAN DO FOR HER.

MOM...

ON TOP OF EVERYTHING ELSE YOU'VE BEEN THROUGH.

IT ISN'T FAIR FOR YOU TO HAVE TO DEAL WITH THIS.

"BUT *HOW* YOU DO WILL DEFINE YOU.

BLEEDING ON THE UPPER RIGHT ABDOMEN IS UNDER CONTROL.

GOOD, THIS GIANT HOLE IN HIS CHEST ISN'T.

BIO-CIRCUITRY EVERYWHERE-- NEED THE SYNAPTIC WELDERS TO CLEAN IT OFF.

"YOU'VE BEEN SO STRONG, STEVE..."

...BUT I KNOW YOU'RE TERRIBLY FRIGHTENED.

I'LL BE LEAVING YOU ALL ALONE...

BUT I KNOW YOU'LL FIND YOUR WAY.

STOP, MOM. YOU NEED TO REST.

THAT'S THE GIFT OF THIS PLACE, THE UNYIELDING SPIRIT OF A FREE PEOPLE.

OPTIMISM IS THE AMERICAN STATE OF BEING.

NO MATTER THE CALAMITY, WE REMAIN SUREFOOTED CONFIDENT OF TOMORROW'S RETURN.

"...IT'S WHY WE CAME HERE, STEVE.

"IT'S WHAT WE WANTED FOR YOU."

THESE TENDRILS ARE FUSED TO HIS NERVOUS SYSTEM, PYM.

TAKE YOUR TIM DOCTOR BANNER

NEVER ALLOW THIS CHALLENGE, THIS GRIEF, TO DEFEAT YOU, STEVE.

GET PAST THIS AND NO MATTER WHAT LIFE THROWS AT YOU-- *YOU'LL OVERCOME IT.*

IN ORDER TO GROW YOU MUST LET GO OF THE PAST.

MOM... PLEASE...

INSIDE THAT SMALL FRAME IS A BIG, STRONG HEART.

A GOOD MAN.

"A STRONG HEART WILL TAKE YOU FURTHER THAN ANY PHYSICAL STRENGTH.

"A STRONG HEART MEANS YOU'LL NEVER QUIT...

"...YOU'LL ALWAYS MAINTAIN THE OPTIMISM OF THIS GREAT NATION."

OKAY, I'M IN. THIS SHOULD LOCATE AND DESTROY ANY OF THE FOREIGN TISSUE.

"YOU CAN'T BE STUCK HERE..."

LIFE IS TOO SHORT TO ALLOW YOURSELF TO BECOME TRAPPED IN ONE CHAPTER.

YOU LEARN WHAT YOU CAN, YOU STAND UP, AND YOU MOVE FORWARD.

HOW CAN I GO FORWARD WITHOUT YOU?

MY LOVE IS IN YOU, ANGEL.

NO MATTER WHERE YOU GO...

TWELVE YEARS?!

AS BEST AS I CAN TELL. YES.

THE CARBON DATE TESTING I RAN ON THE UNIFORM CONFIRMS IT.

YOU DON'T LOOK TWELVE YEARS OLDER.

I HADN'T NOTICED.

A SUPER-SOLDIER SERUM EFFECT WE NEVER THOUGHT MUCH ABOUT.

CONGRATULATIONS, STEVE. IT APPEARS YOU DON'T AGE NORMALLY.

THE ZOLA INFECTION?

ERASED IT AND THE BIO-CIRCUITS WELDED TO HIS NERVOUS SYSTEM.

HE GETS A CLEAN BILL. *PHYSICALLY* ANYWAY.

CAPTAIN, ABOUT AGENT CARTER, I HAVE TO ASK...

WE NEED TO BE CERTAIN THERE WASN'T ANY CHANCE OF SURVIVAL?

I DON'T KNOW WHAT THE FUTURE HOLDS, JET. BUT I'M *HERE* FOR YOU.

I'M GOING TO HELP YOU PUT TOGETHER A *NEW* LIFE.

WHAT IF I PREFER MY *OLD* LIFE?

MY MOTHER ONCE TOLD ME, "IN ORDER TO GROW, YOU MUST LET GO OF THE PAST."

THAT'S JUST WHAT YOU'LL HAVE TO DO.

ARE YOU LECTURING ME ABOUT LETTING GO OF THE PAST WHILE STANDING AMIDST YOUR SHRINE TO IT?

I SEE WHAT YOU MEAN.

A FIRE IN THE RAIN

TWELVE

BROOKLYN, NEW YORK. TODAY.

EVERYTHING HERE...

IT'S ALL SO FOREIGN.

MY FRIENDS ARE LIKE STRANGERS.

CAN'T LET ANYONE KNOW WHAT I'VE BEEN THROUGH.

THAT I'M WEAK.

AND THIS CITY-- THIS WORLD-- IT'S NOT HOME.

HOME IS ANOTHER PLANE OF EXISTENCE.

A PLACE WITH TWO SUNS AND BARREN PURPLE DESERTS.

THE PLACE I LEFT MY FAMILY.

WHERE SHARON GAVE HER LIFE.

IT SHOULD HAVE BEEN MY SACRIFICE THAT STOPPED ZOLA.

I SHOULD BE THERE STILL.

WITH MY SON.

THE SON ZOLA TOOK.

BECAUSE HE KNEW.

KNEW EVEN IF I SURVIVED...

I'D DIE WITH IAN.

STEVE?!

LITTLE HELP?!

AN ASSESSMENT MORE APT NOW THAN BEFORE. THIS PLACE WAS A LIFETIME AGO. HOW CAN I BE STRONG, STAND UP AND SERVE...

...IF I CAN'T LET GO OF WHAT HAPPENED?

IT ISN'T SO CUT AND DRIED.

YOU NEVER FORGET...

...BUT OVER TIME, YOU DO LET GO.

I KNOW HOW HARD IT IS, HOW IMPOSSIBLE IT FEELS. YOU LOVED HER, WE ALL DID...

IT'S MORE THAN JUST SHARON, SAM.

ZOLA'S SON.

I SAVED HIM AS AN INFANT. RAISED HIM AS MY OWN.

SHARON...

SHARON KILLED HIM. TH-THOUGHT SHE WAS PROTECTING ME FROM ONE OF ZOLA'S HENCHMEN AND...

I'M LOST HERE. STRUGGLING TO FIND MEANING...

IN A WORLD THAT HOLDS NONE FOR ME.

ROSVEKISTAN,
ASTERN EUROPE.
UKE ENGAGEMENT
NE 2.

THE DAILY BUGLE'S AS TIGHT AS A DRUM THESE DAYS.

I'D MAKE MORE PANHANDLING.

ROBBIE ISN'T PAYING A RED CENT UNLESS I DELIVER A SCOOP.

NEW FACE OF FREELANCE JOURNALISM.

OU DIG IT UP ST, YOU GET PAID--

KLIKK

KLIKK

--COME IN AN HOUR BEHIND THE NEXT GUY--

--AND YOU DON'T.

BUT THIS?

KLIKK

THIS IS GONNA COST YOU, ROBBIE.

JUST AS SOON AS I CAN LINK TO THE SATELLITE AND GET YOU A TASTE.

PHONE'S SCRAMBLED. NO INTERNET EITHER.

KLIKK

SOMEONE DOESN'T WANT THIS GETTING OUT.

HOW THE HELL IS IT ALL CONNECTED?

DOZENS OF THE WORLD'S RICHEST PEOPLE HAVE BEEN DISAPPEARING.

AND EVERY TRAIL LEADS HERE.

WUPWUPPWUPPWUPP

"AMERICA
DOESN'T
LOSE."

THIRTEEN

WHAT'S IT BEEN, RAN? TWO YEARS?

NOW, I GO TWO YEARS AWAY FROM AN OLD FRIEND, *NO* CALL, *NO* LETTER-- I GET SAD.

I WORRY THE RELATIONSHIP IS *ERODING*.

BUT WHEN I LOSE CONTACT WITH MY *NUMBER ONE AGENT* INFILTRATING MAO'S LITTLE PARTY OVER IN CHINA, WELL, WHEN *THAT* FRIEND GOES QUIET--

--I GET DOWNRIGHT *NERVOUS.*

YOU KNOW THE TIME I INVESTED IN CLIMBING TO MAO'S SIDE, FURY.

I COULDN'T RISK CONTACT.

DO YOU APPRECIATE THE *RISK* I TAKE REPORTING EVEN NOW?

THAT'S A *DODGE*--AND I CAN SMELL, 'EM.

THERE'S *NOTHIN'* YOU'RE LEAVIN' OUT?

I COULDN'T RISK ALERTING MAO.

HMM. SEE, THE WAY I HEAR IT, MAO IS ALREADY BEYOND ALERTED.

RUMOR HAS IT YOU WENT AGAINST HIS ORDERS, PISSED OFF THE SOVIETS.

HE CAST YOU OUT. STRIPPED YOUR RANK.

RAN SHEN IS A *MADMAN,* THEY SAY.

AND COMIN' FROM *THAT* CREW--THAT'S SOMETHIN'.

WORD IS HE MADE A POWER GRAB. OVERREACHED. GOT CAUGHT.

NOW, NOT A WEEK AFTER HE ESCAPES MAO'S RETALIATION, HE SHOWS UP HERE.

YOU ALWAYS WERE A COCKY S.O.B., BUT DID YOU REALLY THINK I WOULDN'T FIND OUT, RAN?

PERHAPS I WANTED YOU TO.

RIGHT. AND NOW YOU'VE GOT US RIGHT WHERE YOU WANT US.

YOU WERE MY CHOICE. SO THIS IS ON MY INFERNAL NOGGIN FOR TRUSTIN' YOU WERE TRUE...

TURNS OUT YOUR BLOOD RUNS PINK.

SO BE IT.

ONLY THING I DON'T KNOW-- WHY THE HELL COME BACK HERE?

TO FULFILL A PROMISE TO A FRIEND

A PROMISE MADE AS YOU LAY DYING, FATHER.

YOU SUFFERED SUCH *INDIGNITY* AT THEIR HANDS.

BUT INSTEAD OF FEELING RAGE AT THE CAPITALISTIC *CORRUPTION* THAT ALLOWED THUGS TO DESCEND ON THE WORKING CLASS...

...ALL YOU WANTED WAS FOR ME TO GROW STRONG, TO FIGHT FOR JUSTICE.

TO PROTECT OTHERS FROM YOUR FATE.

SUCH BLIND FAITH IN THE "AMERICAN DREAM."

A DREAM THAT CRIPPLED YOU UNDER A STRIKEBREAKER'S BATON.

I HOPE YOU'LL UNDERSTAND IF I RESPECTFULLY DECLINE THE INVITATION TO JOIN THIS HALLUCINATION.

I TRIED, FATHER. GAVE MY LIFE OVER TO THE PURSUIT OF THE AMERICAN IDEALS.

A *FANTASY* SHROUDING THE TRUE *EVIL* MACHINATIONS OF THE GREEDY AND RICH IN CONTROL.

A DREAM SOLD TO LABORING MASSES...

...WORKING UNDER THE MISGUIDED ASSUMPTION THAT THOSE IN POWER HAVE THEIR BEST INTERESTS AT HEART.

TRUTH, JUSTICE, AND LIBERTY FOR ALL.

DEEEP

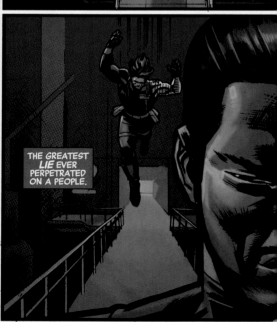

THE GREATEST *LIE* EVER PERPETRATED ON A PEOPLE.

BLAM BLAM BLAM BLAM

TAKE 'EM DOWN!

YOU'VE HURT YOUR OWN CAUSE, SOVIET DOG!

PSHHHHHH

SHOOT TO KILL!

DO NOT LET THAT MAN ESCAPE!

BLAM BLAM

PNK

TNK

SKK

GET THE MEN SCOURING!

WON'T DO ANY GOOD.

THAT GUY WAS TOO GOOD TO NOT HAVE A TIGHT ESCAPE PLAN.

WHO WAS HE AND WHAT THE HELL DID RAN SHEN WANT IN HERE FOR?

NEVER SEEN STEVE LIKE THIS.

EVER.

HE JUST TOOK IT ALL-- PICTURES, COSTUMES-- ALL HIS MEMORABILIA--

AND HE *BURNED* IT?

EVERY. PIECE.

PLAPP

TO BE *FREE* OF SHACKLES.

PLAPP

TO GROW PAST THE *BURDENS* OF HIS OLD LIFE.

PLAPP

HE SHOULD NOT REMAIN TETHERED TO *OLD* AND *USELESS* THINGS.

WELL, THIS *OLD* AND *USELESS* THING HAS KNOWN THE MAN LONG ENOUGH TO KNOW *THIS* IS A SIGN OF *TROUBLE.*

PERHAPS IT THREATENS *YOU, SAM WILSON.* ANOTHER *RELIC.*

NO LONGE THE ONE W KNOWS HI *BEST.*

IT'S MORE THAN SHARON. I'M NOT AT LIBERTY TO SAY ANYTHING ELSE, BUT...

...LET SOMEONE ELSE DEAL WITH WHATEVER THE PROBLEM IS.

STEVE *NEEDS* SOME TIME OFF.

I BELIEVE YOU'RE RIGHT, SAM. BUT THIS SITUATION *DEMANDS* HIS PRESENCE.

THE WORLD *MUST* SEE CAPTAIN AMERICA DEAL WITH NUKE OR WE'RE GOING TO BE LOOKING DOWN THE BARREL OF *WORLD WAR III.*

NUKE?

FORMER SUPER-SOLDIER, FOUGHT IN VIETNAM.

CYBORG WITH EXTREME MENTAL ILLNESS BORN OF A VERSION OF THE SUPER-SOLDIER FORMULA AND HYPER-AMPHETAMINES.

WEAPON VII

HE'S REOPENING THE CONFLICT WE FOUGHT IN NROSVEKISTAN.

HE'S DECIMATING CITIES AND PLANTING AMERICAN FLAGS IN THE RUBBLE.

WE'VE BLACKED OUT THE MEDIA. NO ONE KNOWS-- YET.

WE CAN'T MAINTAIN IT MUCH LONGER.

DEAR GOD. WHAT'S THE INTERNATIONAL REACTION BEEN?

APON VII

BUT THEY DIDN'T COUNT ON SAMANTHA CHAN.

BRAKAKAKAKA

BRAKAKAKK

<HE'S UNSTOPPABLE--!>

BRAKAKAKKAKKA

<RUN!> <THERE'S NO-- YARKK!>

BECAUSE OF YOU-- AMERICANS ARE ASHAMED OF THEMSELVES!

ASHAMED OF OUR BOYS!

I'M AN AMERICAN--

EVERY GREAT NATION SUFFERS A DECLINE--

--THIS MAN IS A LIVING REMINDER OF OUR DARKEST HOUR--

KWUDD

--A RELIC OF AN AMERICA I WASN'T THERE TO HELP.

ONE CHANCE, SOLDIER. **STAND DOWN.**

I'M UNDER ORD FROM TH GENERA

HIS EYES--

--BLANK--

--OUT OF HIS MIND.

NO REASONING WITH HIM--

--TOO POWERFUL TO RISK.

TWUNGG

GIVE IT EVERYTHING I HAVE--

TWUMP

SMELL OF BURNING FLESH HANGS IN THE AIR--

FIGHT THE GAG REFLEX--

THE WRONG SIDE WON THIS WAR.

--GET UP--

STOP HIM--

--BEFORE HIS BODY COUNT GROWS.

<HE'S COMING! READY YOUR--?>

GHRAGHAH!

FWOOOOSH

YERAHAAAAAHH--!

SINKING FEELING IN MY GUT--

--WHISPERING A HARD TRUTH--

"HE'S BEYOND YOU.

"AND NO ONE IS COMING TO HELP."

YOU WEREN'T THE PEOPLE WE SUPPORTED.

BRAKAKAKAKKAAA

IGNORE THE SCREAMS--

--THE SMELL--

GET UP--

--STOP THIS MADMAN.

YOU WEREN'T SUPPOSED TO WIN.

BRAKA KAKA KAKA

BURNING SOLDIER-- TOO FAR GONE.

DEAD AT THE HANDS OF A MAN WITH MY FLAG ON HIS FACE.

DEAD AT THE HANDS OF AN AMERICAN SUPER-SOLDIER.

MADE US LOOK BAD.

MADE THE BOYS LOOK BAD.

EVERY DEAD BODY-- ANOTHER FAMILY THAT'LL SEE THE U.S. AS AN ENEMY.

EVERY DEAD BODY A SIGNPOST THAT WE'VE LOST CONTROL.

‹DEAR GOD...›

NO WAR LOST.

THEY SAY ALL WE OFFER THE WORLD IS WAR--

THEY SAY WE'RE CORRUPTED BY MILITARY AMBITION.

HE'S GOING TO PROVE THEM RIGHT.

FREAK.

BRAKA KAKAKA

PNG

SNK

SNK

HOW MANY HAS HE KILLED?

DON'T THINK ABOUT THAT--

--JUST DO WHATEVER YOU CAN--

GRA-DOOOM

--SAVE THO WHO ARE LE

YOU FIGHT AGAINST YOUR OWN TROOPS?

FOR THESE SWINE?

GET UP--

GET UP, DAMMIT--

MY ORDERS ARE CLEAR, SIR--

NUKE'S **MURDERED** DOZENS OF INNOCENTS.

PLANTED MY FLAG IN THE BODIES.

HOURS NOW.

HOURS TRYING TO STOP HIM.

NOTHING SLOWS HIM DOWN.

PUNTT

AND MY CONTROL IS FADING.

SOMETHING'S UNLEASHING ITSELF.

TWOK

SOMETHING CAGED INSIDE ME--

--SOMETHING **FURIOUS.**

CHOKK

SOME NEW RAGE.

BORN OF GRIEF.

MY MIND IN ANOTHER PLACE.

WUKK

WITH MY DEAD FAMILY.

RAGE MAKES ME SLOPPY.

RAGE ISN'T THE SOLUTION TO THIS--

INTELLECT MIGHT BE.

DEATH TO **ANYONE** IN MY WAY.

MY ORDERS, SIR.

YOU'RE A **PATRIOT,** AGENT SIMPSON.

A **GOOD** SOLDIER.

BUT YOUR ORDERS ARE **BUNK.**

WHY ELSE WOULD I BE HERE TRYING TO **STOP** YOU?

MY ORDERS--

ARE LIES.

LET'S GET YOU HOME, FIND WHOEVER THE HELL IS GIVING THEM, AND TAKE THEM DOWN.

WE'LL GET YOU HELP. A FAIR TRIAL.

FOLLOWING ORDERS...

I WAS JUST--

CHIKK

TWONK

YOU THINK THIS SLAUGHTER HONORS THE DEAD?

THOSE MEN **DIED** FOR THE PEACE YOU'RE DESTROYING.

WHUMPP

DOESN'T THAT MEAN **ANYTHING** TO YOU?!

HOW DARE YOU?!

WHAT DO YOU KNOW ABOUT OUR SACRIFICES, **CIVILIAN?!**

GOD-- OH, GOD--

WHAAAA--!

CAN'T LET YOU DO IT AGAIN.

YOU RUINED LIVES. OUR BOYS CAME HOME TO A COUNTRY THAT *HATED* THEM.

THEY SHOULD'VE COME HOME AS *HEROES*.

I-I'M NOT...I DIDN'T...

THEY FOUGHT AND DIED FOR YOUR FREEDOMS.

AND YOU BETRAYED THEM.

NEVER. AGAIN.

NO--!

TAKE IT.

MAKE A CHOICE.

DO YOU BELIEVE IN FREEDOM OF THE PRESS AS A FUNDAMENTAL RULE...

...OR ONLY WHEN IT'S CONVENIENT TO THOSE IN CHARGE?

WHAT ARE YOUR PRINCIPLES, FALCON?

AND HOW FAR AWAY FROM THEM WILL YOU GO TO UPHOLD THEM?

AN ENVOY WILL BE BY TO COLLECT YOU SOON.

ALL I EVER WANTED...

FOR OUR BOYS...

FOR THE FORGOTTEN.

NICK. DIDN'T EXPECT TO SEE YOU HERE.

I THOUGHT WE HAD TO KEEP THINGS QUIET UNTIL YOU COULD SHOW ME BRINGING HIM IN?

DOESN'T MATTER ANYMORE.

NEWS GOT OUT.

SOME REPORTER MADE IT PAST OUR BLACKOUT ZONE.

AMERICAN OPERATIVES IN NROSVEKISTAN KILL HUNDREDS

UPLOADED THIS ABOUT THREE MINUTES BACK.

THAT REPORTER... YOU TOOK HER CAMERA. ISN'T THAT RIGHT, SAM?

TELL FURY YOU STOPPED HER.

CHINA.

FREEDOM OF THE PRESS CAN BE A DOUBLE-EDGED SWORD.

I DON'T RELISH USING THE FEW REMAINING FIBERS OF AMERICAN INTEGRITY, AMID THE FETID TAPESTRY, AGAINST THEM.

NOR DO I TAKE PLEASURE IN USING THEIR OWN CHAMPIONS TO FURTHER SMEAR THEIR ALREADY *TARNISHED* REPUTATION.

BUT WHEN I AM DONE, THEY WILL BE *BETTER* FOR IT.

AS GERMANY GREW STRONGER IN THE DECADES AFTER THEIR EVIL REICH WAS CRUSHED.

THE CORRUPT INFECTION OF THE CAPITALIST WEST AND ITS CORPORATE MASTERS HAS SPREAD TOO DEEP.

TO HEAL THIS GANGRENOUS LIMB, WE MUST *HACK IT OFF.*

AND TO DO THAT, WE MUST RID OURSELVES OF THEIR *GESTAPO* IN THE SKY.

WE CANNOT CHANGE THE WORLD UNTIL THE SECRET POLICE OF THE EMPIRE FALLS.

FOR HUMANITY TO THRIVE IN A PEACEFUL WORLD...

I WILL NOT BE WORKED TO DEATH HERE.

PLOKK

HNNG--

I WILL BRING AN *ARMY* BACK WITH ME.

I WILL FREE THESE SAD CAPTIVES.

I WILL BRING THIS SLAVE LABOR CAMP *DOWN*.

DINGG

I *WILL* SEE MY FAMILY AGAIN.

"...YOUR FAMILIES' LIVES **DEPEND** ON IT."

THEY CALL ME NUKE...

...BUT I NEVER LIKED THE NAME.

IT'S NOT FITTING, SIR.

I'M A BOOTS ON THE GROUND SOLDIER.

I'M NOT SOME BOMB DETONATED FROM A THOUSAND MILES AWAY.

I FOUGHT WITH OUR BOYS.

I FOLLOW **ORDERS.**

YOU WERE GIVEN SOME BAD ONES, SOLDIER.

DON'T PICK AND CHOSE THE ORDERS WE FOLLOW.

A SOLDIER'S LOYALTIES ARE TO HIS COMMANDING OFFICER...

"...AND THE BOYS IN THE COMPANY.

"PUT LIFE AND LIMB ON THE LINE WHEN COMMAND SAYS SO.

"*WHEREVER* THEY SAY.

"THE HOT JUNGLES.

"THAT'S WHERE I SPENT MY TIME, SIR.

"NOT IN AN OFFICE LOOKING AT A BUTTON.

"I HEARD OUR BOYS SCREAM.

"WATCHED THEM BLEED.

"LOOKING MY ENEMY IN THE *EYES*."

THEY CALLED ME *NUKE* FROM BEFORE I CAN REMEMBER.

IT'S JUST NOT FITTING.

THEY CALLED YOU THAT BECAUSE THAT'S WHAT YOU WERE *EXPECTED* TO BE, AGENT SIMPSON. I'VE READ YOUR FILES.

THEY EXPECTED YOU TO SCORCH THE EARTH AND WIN THE WAR--NO MATTER THE BODY COUNT.

BUT WHEN FIRST DEPLOYED, YOU DIDN'T DO WHAT THEY EXPECTED YOU TO, AGENT SIMPSON.

YOU WERE MORE INTERESTED IN *PROTECTING* AMERICAN SOLDIERS THAN *KILLING* THE ENEMY.

YOU WERE BLOWN TO BITS DOING JUST THAT.

AND FOR YOUR SERVICE THE WEAPON PLUS PROGRAM PLEDGED TO REBUILD YOU.

TO CREATE THE NEXT GENERATION OF *SUPER-SOLDIER.*

AND THEY DID.

BUT THEY WENT TOO FAR--REWIRED YOUR BRAIN.

MADE SURE YOU WERE *INCAPABLE* OF IGNORING YOUR ORDERS.

YOU'RE A *VICTIM* OF SOME *EVIL* MEN WHO TWISTED YOUR HONOR.

AGENT LAMIA HERE, HER FATHER WAS ONE OF THE SOLDIERS YOU WERE NEARLY KILLED SAVING.

I BROUGHT HER ALONG TO REMIND YOU OF WHO YOU ONCE WERE.

IT'S TRUE.

I WOULDN'T BE HERE IF IT WEREN'T FOR YOU, AGENT SIMPSON.

IT WAS MY FATHER'S PLATOON YOU NEARLY DIED PROTECTING.

YOU WERE HIS CAPTAIN AMERICA.

YOU WERE A GOOD SOLDIER.

YOU SERVED YOUR COUNTRY PROUDLY. AND WITH SOME REHABILITATION, I THINK YOU CAN SERVE HER AGAIN.

BUT, RIGHT NOW, I NEED FOR YOU TO UNDERSTAND--

YOU'VE BEEN *LIED* TO.

SIR, *NO,* SIR.

THE GENERAL ONLY DEPLOYS ME WHEN MY COUNTRY'S PROSPERITY AND SAFETY ARE AT RISK.

THE GENERAL TOLD ME NOT TO TRUST ANYONE ELSE UNTIL WE'VE WON--

THERE'S *NOTHING* TO WIN.

THE WAR *IS* OVER, SON.

AND IT'S TIME TO COME *HOME* FROM IT.

I KNOW HOW FRIGHTENING THAT CAN BE TO HEAR.

IT MEANS YOU TO HAVE TO COME BACK.

IT MEANS YOU HAVE TO REJOIN A WORLD THAT IS IN NO WAY FAMILIAR TO YOU.

TO SMILE AND PRETEND THAT EVERYTHING IS NORMAL.

BUT IN ORDER TO GROW YOU MUST LET GO OF THE PAST.

THAT'S THE HARDEST PART OF OUR DUTY, AGENT SIMPSON.

CAN YOU ACCEPT *THOSE* ORDERS?

WE KNOW IT WASN'T YOUR FAULT.

THE PEOPLE WHO SET YOU TO DO THIS *TERRIBLE* THING--THIS IS ON *THEM*.

BUT WE *NEED* TO KNOW *WHO* IT WAS.

BECAUSE OF WHAT YOU'VE DONE, THERE'S NO EASY WAY TO SAY THIS--WE'RE LOOKING AT A POTENTIAL FOR *WAR* HERE.

WE DESPERATELY NEED TO KNOW WHO DID THIS.

I...

I'LL TRY...

...I'LL TELL YOU EVERYTHING I CAN REMEMBER.

THAT'S ALL WE'RE ASKING, AGENT SIMPSON.

HELP US DEFUSE THIS BOMB.

FAR TOO LATE FOR THAT, CAPTAIN.

WEAPON MINUS, GUNGNIR, ALL THE SECRET CRIMES OF YOUR EMPIRE WILL SOON BE TURNED UPON YOU.

"THE DECIMATION OF THE WEST AND THEIR SECRET POLICE IS INEVITABLE."

S.H.I.E.L.D.'S HUB STATION, THE GRAND CANYON.

GOOD WORK, CAP.

YOU GOT THROUGH TO HIM.

THEY SAY WE TEACH BEST WHAT WE MOST NEED TO LEARN.

WE ALL HAVE TO COME BACK FROM OUR OWN WARS, STEVE.

ROOKLYN.

DAMNED NIGHTMARE.

WHAT THE HELL DO YOU THINK THEY DID TO NUKE?

MORE IMPORTANTLY **WHO** DID IT?

THAT'S AN ANSWER FURY AND HIS TEAM HAD BETTER GET OUT OF HIM--AND **SOON.**

I JUST CAN'T FIGURE OUT THE ANGLE.

SEEMS SIMPLE ENOUGH-- DEFAME AN AMERICAN SUPER HERO, DEFAME AMERICA.

TO MAKE IT LOOK LIKE THIS ATTACK WAS SOMETHING I SUPPORTED.

MAYBE... MAYBE THAT'S ALL IT IS.

BUT YOU DON'T THINK SO.

I THINK WHEN SOMEBODY ORCHESTRATES SOMETHING THAT PERFECTLY--GOING TO THE TROUBLE OF COLLECTING AND MIND-WARPING SOMEONE AS DANGEROUS AS NUKE...

I CAN'T HELP BUT THINK THAT THERE'S A **DEEPER** GAME AFOOT.

AS USUAL, YOU'VE GOT A GOOD EYE FOR **DETAIL.**

BUT STEP ONE IS CLEARLY A SMEAR CAMPAIGN.

SLANDER IS THE MOST EFFECTIVE AND EASIEST WAY TO DESTROY SOMEONE.

NO ONE READS ARTICLES ANYMORE--THEY READ **HEADLINES.**

EITHER WAY, I'M IN NO SHAPE FOR THIS.

ALMOST MADE A TERRIBLE MISTAKE OUT THERE. IF YOU HADN'T STOPPED ME...

YOU'VE BEEN THROUGH A LOT, STEVE.

GET SOME REST...

"...I'LL SEE IF I CAN'T HELP GET THROUGH TO NUKE."

SIR, I'VE TOLD YOU ALL I CAN REMEMBER, SIR. THE REDS... THEY CLOUD MY HEAD AFTER...

YOU'RE TIRED, I KNOW. FULL OF THOSE DRUGS.

WE'LL START BACK OVER IN THE MORNING.

SEE IF WE CAN'T CRACK THOSE MIND BLOCKS THEY PUT INSIDE YOU.

WHAT YOU SAID IN THE COPTER, AGENT, WAS IT TRUE?

DID I SAVE YOUR FATHER?

YES, SIR.

PFC FRANKLIN LAMIA. HIS COMPANY WAS FLANKED, THE LOCATION GIVEN AWAY BY AN OFFICER KLUTZ.

WHAT THE--?!

GHA--
GHRAGHH--!

DEPLOY THE DRAGON...

"THE ESTABLISHMENT'S WORST NIGHTMARE CAME TRUE.

"DR. MINDBUBBLE, THE PSYCHEDELIC SUPER-SOLDIER, WAS BORN."

TRIPPY.

TO BE CONTINUED...

#15 VARIANT BY FRANCESCO MATTINA

CAPTAIN AMERICA

#12 LEGO VARIANT BY **LEONEL CASTELLANI**

#11

IRON NAIL DESIGNS BY CARLOS PACHECO

CAPTAIN AMERICA #11
script by RICK REMENDER
pencils by CARLOS PACHECO • inks by KLAUS JANSON

PAGE 1

1 - OPEN ON A FLASHBACK - NY - 1935: Steve's mom is dying, Very sick, SHE SITS IN THE KITCHEN, IN A BLANKET. Behind her STEVE and the DOCTOR talk. Steve is a young man here, early teens, thin, weak looking, very poor.

SEE ISSUES 1-3 FOR REFERENCE OF THE ROGER'S HOME FORM THIS ERA.

DOCTOR

I'm sorry, Steve.

2 - IN ON STEVE, now turning and looking at his Mom as the doctor clearly gives him bad news. Steve's face is sad. The doctor is offering his sympathies.

DOCTOR

There's nothing left I can do for her.

3 - The doctor is putting his hat on, Steve still looking at his mother. Steve is shattered, fighting tears.

4 - The doctor leaves, young Steve approaches from behind his Mother and puts a hand on her shoulder.

STEVE

Mom…

SARAH ROGERS

On top of everything else you've been through.

5 - STEVE'S POV - Sarah puts her hand on top of Steve's hand as she turns and looks up at us/Steve. She looks sick, thin, pale, and dying but she still manages a big reassuring smile.

SARAH ROGERS

It isn't fair for you to have to deal with this

PAGE 2

1 - CUT TO - NOW - SHIELD LAB - STEVE ROGERS IN A HIGH-TECH SHIELD LAB - CAP is on an angled lab table, one side is BRUCE BANNER, on the other is HANK PYM, both are operating on Cap. Cap has his shirt off revealing his bare chest, and the terrible scar in the center of it where he cut the Zola face out of his own chest. He's covered in scars, scabs, wounds, blood, dirt--he's been through hell.

SARAH ROGERS

"But how you do will define you."

BRUCE BANNER

Bleeding on the upper right abdomen under control.

HANK PYM (BG)

Good, this giant hole in his chest isn't.

Bio circuitry everywhere--need the synaptic welders to clean it off.

SARAH ROGERS (CAP)

You've been so strong, Steve…

2 - CUT TO - FLASHBACK: Sarah Rogers is bundled in a blanket on the couch now, very sick. Steve is entering the living room with some steaming soup in a bowl.

SARAH ROGERS

…but I know you're terribly frightened.

STEVE

Stop, Mom. You need to rest.

SARAH ROGERS

Leaving you all alone…

But I know you'll find your way.

3 - Sarah and Steve sit on the couch, she's looking him in the eyes, smiling. Steve has set the soup on the table in front of her.

SARAH ROGERS

That's the gift of this place, the unyielding spirit of a free people.

Optimism is the American state of being.

No matter the calamity, we remain surefooted, confident of tomorrows return…

4 - CUT TO - NOW - STEVE ROGERS IN A HIGH-TECH SHIELD LAB - HIS CHEST IS BEING OPERATED ON BY BANNER, it's a mess, scarred up badly, puss and blood. This is the injury Steve got when he cut the Zola screen out of his chest.

SARAH ROGERS (CAP)

"…It's why we came here, Steve.

"It's what we wanted for you."

BRUCE BANNER

These tendrils are fused to his nervous system, Pym.

PYM

Take your time.

5 - CUT TO - FLASHBACK: Steve's mom is dying. Very sick. She sits up, looking at her son in the eyes.

SARAH ROGERS

Never allow this challenge, this grief, to defeat you, Steve.

Get past this and no matter what life throws at you-- you'll overcome it.

PAGE 3

1 - On Steve, weeping, holding his Mother's trembling hand.

SARAH ROGERS

In order to grow you must let go of the past.

STEVE (WEAK/WAVY)

Mom… please…

SARAH ROGERS

Inside that small frame is a big strong heart.

A good man.

2 - CUT TO - NOW - STEVE ROGERS IN A HIGH-TECH SHIELD LAB - Pym is sealing up the chest wound with a high tech gizmo. Banner helping.

SARAH ROGERS (CAP)

"A strong heart will take you further than any physical strength.

"A strong heart means you'll never quit…

3 - Pym injects a strange red liquid into Steve's chest.

SARAH ROGERS (CAP)

"…You'll always maintain the optimism of this great nation."

PYM

Okay, I'm in.

This should locate and destroy any of the foreign tissue.

SARAH ROGERS

"You can't be stuck here…"

4 - CUT TO - FLASHBACK: Steve's mom is leaning forward now to look her boy in the eyes.

SARAH ROGERS

Life is too short to allow yourself to become trapped in one chapter.

You learn what you can, you stand up, and you move forward.

STEVE

How can I go forward without you?

5 - She smiles so warmly at him. Tears streaming down both of their faces now. Her eyes are full of pride for her skinny and sickly son.

SARAH ROGERS

My love is in you, angel.

No matter where you go…

PAGE 4

ALL PAGE WIDE PANELS

1 - CUT TO - MOM'S FUNERAL - SNOWY DAY - STEVE'S ALONE, IN AN INEXPENSIVE SUIT OF THE ERA. ALL HIS FAMILY IS DEAD. NO ONE ELSE AT THE FUNERAL.

SARAH ROGERS (CAP)

"I'll always be in your heart."

2 - ON YOUNG STEVE, watching the casket be

lowered. Alone, his family is dead. This skinny kid will face the world alone. He holds a flower. He weeps.

3 - CUT TO - INT. SHIELD HUB - CAP is being operated on, another wound sewn shut by Pym. He is in bad shape.

BANNER

He's been through hell. I'm frankly surprised he survived.

PYM

Think about whom you're talking about.

BANNER

Yeah, but even for him, I know Steve's strong, but this…

4 - CUT TO - THE FUNERAL - STEVE DROPS A FLOWER ON THE CASKET.

BANNER (CAP)

"…I don't know how he stood up after taking this kind of a beating."

5 - PULL UP AND OUT - YOUNG STEVE WALKS AWAY. The snow drifts down as his mother is buried.

BANNER (CAP)

"Where does any one man get that kind of courage?"

PAGE 5

I - CUT TO - EXT. SHIELD LAND BASE THE HUB - DAY - WE SAW THIS BASE IN UNCANNY AVENGERS #1, it is buried in the side of a dessert canyon's red rock.

MARIA HILL (INSIDE)

Twelve years?!

2 - INT. SHIELD HUB - LATER - CAP is cleaned up now, shaven, sitting up in a medical bed, on one side is BRUCE BANNER, on the other is HANK PYM, both are caring for Cap. In front of Cap is MARIA

HILL, listening to his incredible story. Cap has his shirt off revealing his bare chest, and the multiple places he's wrapped up in gauze, it's crazy, the man has been through Hell. He's COVERED IN BAND AIDS AND GAUZE.

CAPT. AMERICA

As best as I can tell.

Yes.

HANK PYM

The carbon date testing I ran on the uniform confirms it.

3 - MARIA HILL GETS CLOSE, looking closely at the cleanly shaven and fixed up Steve Rogers face, looking for wrinkles.

MARIA HILL

You haven't aged.

CAPT. AMERICA

I hadn't noticed.

4 - On Banner and Pym, they mess about with holographic controls and high tech doo-dads, instruments connected to Steve, doing his vitals etc.

BRUCE BANNER

A super-soldier serum affect we never thought much about.

HANK PYM

Congratulations Steve. It appears you don't age.

(CONT'D)

5 - Maria turns to Banner and Pym.

MARIA HILL

The Zola infection?

BRUCE BANNER

Erased it and the bio circuits welded to his nervous system.

PYM

He gets a clean bill. Physically anyway.

6 - ON MARIA HILL, TROUBLED, LOOKING UP.

MARIA HILL

Captain, about Agent Carter, I have to ask…

We need to be certain there wasn't any chance of survival?

7 - Steve looks down, silent. EVERYONE IS SILENT.

PAGE 6

1 - Maria places a caring hand on Cap's arm, she smiles warmly at him.

MARIA HILL

I'm sorry, but we needed to be sure.

My deepest condolences.

CAPT. AMERICA

No need to apologize, Maria.

MARIA HILL

Twelve years… I can't even imagine what you've been through.

2 - On Steve, lost in thought, a million miles away.

MARIA HILL (OP)

I want to keep you close, for observation.

MARIA HILL (OP)

So you can talk to someone about it all, about Sharon…

3 - Steve looks away, lost in thought.

4 - SAME SHOT - STEVE LOOKS UP AND FORCES A SMILE. Pretends he's okay all of a sudden.

CAPT. AMERICA

I'll feel better fulfilling my duties, Commander Hill.

Getting back to it.

5 - On Maria, very worried.

MARIA HILL

Of Course, Captain.

I didn't mean to suggest otherwise…

6 - Maria walks out of the room.

MARIA HILL

And don't worry, Steve. Consider this top level classified.

Highly. None of this leaves the room.

HANK PYM

Zip.

BRUCE BANNER

Zilch.

PAGE 7

1 - CAP TURNS TO BANNER. They can all tell he's hurt, but he acts strong.

CAPT. AMERICA

Where's Jet?

BRUCE BANNER

She proved… less than amicable. Rude even.

CAPT. AMERICA

Where is she now?

2 - CUT TO - EST. SHIELD INTERROGATION ROOM - MODERN NICK FURY stands calmly, JET BLACK is in shackles, chained to the floor. She is still wearing her battle costume, she is still battle worn from issue 10's climax.

BRUCE BANNER

"With the only equally as disagreeable person I know.

Who isn't gamma irradiated anyway."

NICK FURY

I don't like to dance around things, Jet.

You see, here, adult people, you waste their time-- they just move on.

If I move on, you move to a jail cell, remember?

3 - On Jet, evil, smiling coldly at Nick, she is top lit to add noir mood.

NICK FURY (OP)

I don't know much about where you come from, not yet I do not, but here on Earth--oh, it's a busy world.

We all have lots to be doing.

4 - Two shot - Nick paces, Jet looks straight ahead.

NICK FURY

Now, Captain America vouched for you, promised you'd be forthcoming.

You're lucky. Cap's a high value advocate here.

NICK FURY

Your Father, on the other hand, is among the very worst human beings that this planet has ever produced.

5 - Fury leans, fists on the table, getting himself closer to Jet.

NICK FURY (STROKED)

So, before I sign off on granting THE DAUGHTER OF ARNIM ZOLA access to MY WORLD--I'm going to know a BIT about her.

SFX

KLAMM

PAGE 8

1 - NICK FURY LEANS IN CLOSER, getting right in Jet's face.

NICK FURY

And make no mistake--that's where you are now, Princess.

My world.

And my world is a sunny and happy place provided you play by the rules.

If you don't...

2 - Nick turns around picking up a notebook and a pen off of the desk.

NICK FURY

Well, I can make it a dark place full of missed opportunity and grave remorse.

So.

Now…

3 - Nick Fury licks the tip of a pen, he holds a notebook, he's shooting Jet a sly look as he prepares to take notes.

NICK FURY

List your super powers.

Captain America tells me you're a test tube super warrior, a real gifted fighter.

What kind of fighting?

4 - Jet looks up, cold.

JET

Release me and I will show you the might of my TACHYON FU.

My bare skin can read the near future keeping me ahead of any opponent.

5 - Two shot - Jet and Nick.

NICK FURY

Ladies skin can read the future.

That's a pretty great power, Miss Black.

What else?

JET

Infinite Omniscenses.

6 - On Jet, looking up, evil.

JET

I can smell, hear, and even taste things hundreds of miles away.

However, when I'm using any one sense at omni level, all others are turned off.

NICK FURY (OP)

Nothing's perfect.

PAGE 9

1 - Behind Nick we angle on Jet.

FURY

What can you hear? How far can you hear it?

JET

I can an insect on the other side of the world. I can hear and decipher digital transmissions.

I can hear your heart, strong and level.

I can hear the blood flowing inside your brain.

2 - CLOSER ON JET, looking up at Nick Fury, she is deadly, seductive, and clever.

JET

Flowing to the section related to attraction.

3 - CLOSER STILL ON JET, sexy, manipulative, smart as a whip. SMILING.

JET

You tie up women, interrogate and break them down.

You tell yourself its just part of your job, but that's not all, is it?

There's something else, another reason.

4 - CUT TO FURY - A BIT NERVOUS, curious, caught off guard.

NICK FURY

What would that be?

5 - Tight on Jet, looking up, deadly, sexy.

JET

It gets you off.

PAGE 10

1 - CAP ENTERS THE ROOM, breaking the moment, smiling at Nick. Cap looks wounded and tired, but clean and fresh in his all-new Captain America outfit.

CAPT. AMERICA

Hope I'm not interrupting?

2 - Cap would like a word with Jet alone. She is smiling devilishly at Nick Fury who looks angrily at her.

JET

Mr. Fury and I were just getting acquainted.

CAPT. AMERICA

Okay. Come on. We're leaving.

FURY

I'd feel safer if I could spend a few days with her--

3 - Fury leaves. Shooting Jet a cold look. Jet smiles to him warmly.

JET

It was nice meeting you, Agent Fury.

CAPT. AMERICA

She'll be safe with me, Nick. I promise.

FURY

Truth, Steve…

4 - CUT TO - EXT. SHIELD LAND BASE THE HUB - SUNSET - Captain America and Jet flying away from the base in a classic SHIELD FLYING CAR.

FURY (CAP)

"…It isn't her safety I'm worried about."

CAPT. AMERICA

What did you tell him, Jet?

5 - On Cap, driving. Jet sits next to him.

JET

Most everything.

Nothing about Ian.

As we agreed.

PAGE 11

1 - She turns and looks away, lost on the memory of her brother and father.

JET

My family is dead.

JET

Captive in another world where nothing is familiar.

CAPT.

The uncertainty is terrible.

I can remember the feeling.

2 - EXT. OF THE CAR - it rockets over a forested mountain range.

JET

What will happen to me now? Where will I stay?

CAPT. AMERICA

With me.

Until we can get you settled into a normal human life.

We'll get you some help dealing with the trauma.

3 - Steve looks ahead, lost in thought. Jet turns to him, coy, sad.

JET

What about your trauma? Ian, he was a son to you.

I can only imagine the pain. If want to unburden yourself, I'd be willing to listen…

4 - Silent on Steve driving. Close on Cap, dead inside, a man who lost a son. The setting sun outside adds a beauty to this somber moment.

5 - Jet looks out the other side of the window, neither have anything to say.

JET

I prefer the silence as well.

PAGE 12

1 - CUT TO - SKYLINE OF NROSVEKISTAN - AFTERNOON - SNOWING OUTSIDE - THIS IS A FICTIONS EASTERN EUROPEAN NATION that has been through a number of wars. It's in rough shape, very poor. (We saw this nation designed in Venom #1, ask me for ref). It's a winter day, SNOWING OUTSIDE.

LOC CAP

Nrosvekistan

2 - CUT TO - STREET LEVEL - A man fills a stand with produce for sale. Other pedestrians move around, some women shopping, a drunk stumbles, etc.

3 - THE PRODUCE MAN watches as the SHOPPING WOMEN DROP THEIR BAGS IN SHOCK at something they see down the road. We can't see what yet.

NUKE (OP)

Doesn't matter how much good we've done in the region.

4 - THE GROCER TURNS to see NUKE marching calmly down the center of the dilapidated and war torn street of this ravaged city. Nuke is carrying a large duffle bag full with a giant gun, but we don't want to telegraph that here. It's just a big US MILITARY ISSUE DUFFLE BAG full of something.

NOTES: Agent Simpson: Codenamed Nuke. Project Rebirth. NUKE: skin contains several kinds of plastics. Doesn't burn. Is tough. Skeleton and muscles, only part human. Sergeant Simpson.

NUKE

You still hate us.

5 - PULL OUT WIDE - The citizens all around the street stop and look at the crazy American. Nuke, cold, walking and looking straight ahead. Snow drifts down. Everyone is curious about this.

NUKE

Hate our freedom.

Hate our values.

Hate our God.

PAGE 13

1 - Nuke stops in the center of town and drops the large duffel bag. A man leads a think old horse pulling half of a VW Bug. Another shopkeeper comes out of his shop. People are sanding and listening to this crazy man.

NUKE

Our boys gave their lives here.

Our boys died defending you people from yourselves.

2 - Nuke puts a hand in a pouch on his belt.

NUKE

Those who survived came home forgotten.

No parades.

3 - Nuke looks in his hand to see three pills, red, white and blue.

NUKE

They call what happened here a loss for the U.S.

4 - On his face - He tosses the pills in his mouth.

NUKE

"A war we rushed into and lost."

5 - Nuke grimaces, gritting his teeth, like a junkie who just got a fix.

SFX (BY TEETH)

KKRICHH

6 - Nuke stands tall at attention, his veins are popping out. His face is clenched.

NUKE

But we don't lose.

War here just went on pause--YOU HEAR ME?!

PAGE 14

1 - Nuke is enraged, standing at attention, screaming like Henry Rollins, red in the face, neck bursting with veins. People are scared now, beginning to move away.

NUKE (STROKED/BIG)

THE WAR ISN'T OVER!

You thought we cut and run back home?!

Left our boys to rot for nothing?!

2 - He bends over, reaching back into the duffle bag.

NUKE

That's not American.

3 - NUKE pulls out a GIANT 80S ACTION HERO STYLE MACHINE GUN. The ostentatious kind we saw in PREDATOR.

NUKE

We finish what we start.

We clean our own dishes.

4 - IMPACT - NUKE OPENS FIRE AT US, big classic Nuke hate on his face, opening up in to civilian population off panel.

NUKE

And we don't lose wars.

SFX

BRAKKA-BRAKKA-BRAKKA-

PAGE 15

1 - CUT TO - CAPTAIN AMERICA'S BASE HOME - CLOUDY EVENING - CAP'S FLYING SHIELD CAR HOVERS, IT IS APPROACHING HIS HOME. This base is new, so design it to last. Simple looking red brick apartment building or warehouse in BROOKLYN.

LOC CAP

Brooklyn

CAPT. AMERICA

2 - CLOSER ON THE EXT. BUILDING - FLYING CAR ENTERS A WALL THAT IS A HOLOGRAM FIELD allowing the car to pass right into the building.

CAPT. AMERICA

Hold on.

Don't worry, the wall is a--

JET

Hologram.

3 - INT. CAP'S GARAGE - THE FLYING CAR IS
LANDED, Jet and Cap getting out. We see his other
vehicles here, the Cap motorcycle and some jet packs
on the wall that stark made for him. They are designed
like his new outfit.

JET

I can see.

4 - JET FOLLOWS CAP, they walk through the garage,
towards the entrance to the main room.

JET

This is your home?

CAPT. AMERICA

It was.

PAGE 16-17

1 - DOUBLE PAGE WIDE IMPACT EST. INT. OPEN
PLANNED HOMEBASE OF CAPTAIN AMERICA.
All around them in this rustic, open planned room
is CAP'S OWN PERSONAL MUSEUM. WWII
memorabilia, his various shields, framed images of him
with Various ages of the Avengers. Grab one team
shot form each of the most famous teams from each
decade. The room is plastered with relics, pictures
of Cap with Bucky for the bond drive, propaganda
images of Cap and Torch, A big war time poster of
the Invaders rushing into action, newspaper clippings
from the era etc. In the center of the room is an
old dusty boxing ring, punching bag, etc. This is like
CAPTAIN AMERICA'S BATCAVE, an old and dusty
gym/museum.

CAPT. AMERICA

A million years ago.

2 - He silently shows Jet her new home. She looks at
all the old WWII Cap memorabilia, toys, war bond
posters, lunch boxes, decoder rings, all kinds of Cap
memorabilia.

JET

These proclamations of past victories, they are
important to you?

CAP

Yes.

3 - Cap stops and looks at the big image of him leading
the Invaders in WWII.

CAP

They used to be.

4 - Steve walks on, towards his desk. He walks past
his memories, walls covered, a room full of his WWII
memorabilia. The room is plastered with relics, pics,
newspaper clippings etc.

JET

When I think of Father and Ian I feel a pained
longing…

CAPT. AMERICA

Mourning.

5 - STEVE STOPS AT HIS OLD DESK. It's an old
WWII era wooden desk, on it we see an old picture
of Steve with the original Nick Fury and another of
Sharon Carter. CAP'S ANSWERING MACHINE IS
BLINKING.

CAPT. AMERICA

Grief at the loss of someone you cared for.

6 - CLOSE ON THE ANSWERING MACHINE:

CAPT. AMERICA

MISSED CALL: SHARON CARTER

PAGE 18

1 - Cap ignores it, turns to Jet; she is looking around at
the wall full of Cap memories and memorabilia.

CAPT. AMERICA

I don't know what the future holds, Jet. But I'm here
for you.

I'm going to help you put together a new life.

2 - Jet turns away, frightened, worried.

JET

What if I prefer my old life?

CAPT. AMERICA

My mother once told me, "In order to grow you must
let go of the past."

That's just what you'll have to do.

3 - Jet looks at Steve like he's a hypocrite.

JET

Are you lecturing me about letting go of the past while standing in your shine to it?

4 - SAME SHOT - SHE THEN TURNS TO LOOK AT THE MUSEUM OF CAP AL OVER THE WALL NEXT TO THEM.

5 - PULL WAY BACK WIDE - JET AND CAP STAND LOOKING AT THIS LARGE ROOM FULL OF CAP memorabilia; posters, framed newspaper articles, old shields, pictures of the Invaders, pictures of Steve with Nomad, with Sharon, With Bucky, With the Avengers from all the most famous eras. Newspaper article is framed: Daily Bugle: Torch kills Hitler. War is over. Bucky's original costume is dressed on a mannequin. Nomad's in on another. This is a museum of the life and times of Captain America.

CAPT. AMERICA

I see what you mean.

PAGE 19

1 - CUT TO - ROOFTOP OF CAP'S BUILDING/ BASE - IT'S BEGUN TO RAIN - Steve and Jet on the rooftop of his building, Brooklyn all around them. Grey clouds swirl. There is a pile of stuff in front of them, we can't see it; it's silhouetted.

2 - CLOSER ON JET AND CAP LOOKING DOWN at SOMETHING WE CAN'T SEE YET. Cap looks calm and at peace.

3 - Cap turns and looks at Jet, he's looking for reassurance.

JET

Go on.

4 - Cap looks back down, the rain has really picked up now.

5 - Cap lights a match.

6 - Cap holds the match up, looking at it, thinking.

PAGE 20

EVEN SIZED PAGE WIDE HORIZONTAL PANELS

1 - STEVE DROPS THE MATCH IN THE PILE OF ALL THE MEMORABILIA WE SAW IN HIS BASE. IT'S ALL IN A BIG PILE IN FRONT OF HIM. MAYBE IT'S PILED IN A COUPLE OF METAL GARBAGE CANS. WHATEVER SELLS IT BEST. HE'S BURNING HIS PAST.

2 - FRONT ON CAPTAIN AMERICA AND JET, ILLUMINATED BY THE FIRE, standing in front of the pile of burning boxes of old photos and stuff.

3 - PULL OUT - CAPTAIN AMERICA AND JET, ILLUMINATED BY THE FIRE, standing in front of the pile of burning boxes of old photos and stuff.

4 - PULL OUT FURTHER - RAIN COMING DOWN, the fires builds, growing hirer, fighting the rain. Steve repeats something his mom taught him.

5 - PULL OUT FURTHER STILL, WE'RE VERY WIDE AND FAR NOW, all we see are the silhouettes of the skyline and one building with a small fire burning in the rain. A black plume of smoke drifting upwards.

6 - A PANEL SIZED WHITE SPACE FOR STORY TITLE/CREDITS: FIRE IN THE RAIN

#13 LAYOUTS
BY NIC KLEIN

DATE DUE

MAR 1 7 2018			

F
Remender, Rick
Captain America: Loose Nuke